'DO YOU STILL MISS
YOUR EX-HUSBAND?'

'YES . . . BUT MY AIM
IS IMPROVING.'

'DO YOU STILL MISS YOUR EX-HUSBAND?'

'YES . . . BUT MY AIM IS IMPROVING.'

Quotes from Women on Top

Jasmine Birtles

Michael O'Mara Books Limited

First published in 1996 by
Michael O'Mara Books Limited
9 Lion Yard, Tremadoc Road,
London SW4 7NQ

A CIP catalogue record for this book is available from
the British Library.

ISBN 1-85479-640-2
Printed and bound by Cox & Wyman,
Reading
10, 9, 8, 7, 6, 5, 4, 3, 2, 1

CONTENTS

WOMEN ON TOP

Madonna: I'm tough, ambitious, and I know exactly what I want. If that makes me a bitch, okay.

Joan Collins: It was George Hamilton who said the immortal line, 'Joan, better to be a shrewd businesswoman than a screwed actress.'

Eleanor Roosevelt: Nobody can make you feel inferior without your consent.

Abigail Adams: Remember, all men would be tyrants if they could. If particular care and attention is not paid to the ladies we are determined to foment a Rebellion, and will not hold ourselves bound by any Laws in which we have no voice, or Representation.

Glenda Jackson: If I'm too strong for some people, that's their problem.

Liz Winstead: I think, therefore I'm single.

Gloria Steinem: Some of us are becoming the men we wanted to marry.

Betty Grable: There are two reasons why I'm in show business, and I'm standing on both of them.

Mary Little: There is no pleasure in having nothing to do; the fun is in having lots to do and not doing it.

Mary Norton: I'm no lady; I'm a member of Congress, and I'll proceed on that basis.

Maxine Waters: I have a right to my anger, and I don't want anybody telling me I shouldn't be, that it's not nice to be, and that something's wrong with me because I get angry.

Mother Jones: Get it right, I'm not a humanitarian. I'm a hell-raiser.

Sophie Tucker: I've been rich
and I've been poor; rich is better.

Susan Faludi: Self-esteem
is the basis for feminism because
self-esteem is based on defining
yourself and believing in that
definition. Self-esteem is
regarding yourself as a grown-up.

Fran Lebowitz: Success didn't spoil me; I've always been insufferable.

Gertrude Stein: Besides Shakespeare and me, who do you think there is?

Osa Johnson: A woman that's too soft and sweet is like tapioca pudding - fine for them as like it.

Mitsuye Yamada: We need to raise our voices a little more, even as they say to us, 'This is so uncharacteristic of you.'

Patricia Schroeder (*Congresswoman*): I have a brain and a uterus, and I use both.

Sally Kempton: I became a feminist as an alternative to becoming a masochist.

Jill Ruckelshaus: It occurred to me when I was thirteen and wearing white gloves and Mary Janes and going to dancing school, that no one should have to dance backwards all their lives.

Barbara Walters: Trust your gut.

Katharine Hepburn: I don't care what is written about me so long as it isn't true.

Elizabeth Cady Stanton: I think if women would indulge more freely in vituperation, they would enjoy ten times the health they do. It seems to me they are suffering from repression.

Sharon Stone: My fame has enabled me to torture more formidable men.

Tillie Olsen: Be critical. Women have the right to say: 'This is surface, this falsifies reality, this degrades'.

Aung San Suu Kyi: If you give in to intimidation, you'll go on being intimidated.

Hedda Hopper: I wasn't allowed to speak while my husband was alive, and since he's been gone no one has been able to shut me up.

Jane Bryant Quinn: Even more than the Pill, what has liberated women is that they no longer need to depend on men economically.

Naomi Wolf: The more liberated women become - economically, politically, and personally - the more erotic we are. Freedom is a lot sexier than dependency.

Susan Faludi: My goal is to be accused of being strident.

Rebecca West: People call me a feminist whenever I express sentiments that differentiate me from a doormat or a prostitute.

DO WHAT *I* WANT

Roseanne: The thing women have got to learn is that nobody gives you power. You just take it.

Bette Davis: I have eyes like a bullfrog, a neck like an ostrich and limp hair. You have to be good to survive with that equipment.

Margaret Chase Smith:
When people keep telling you
that you can't do a thing you kind
of like to try it.

Julie Andrews:
(to Rock Hudson)
Remember, *I'm* the leading lady.

Madonna: Listen, everyone is
entitled to my opinion.

Barbara Bush: I'll do anything you want, but I won't dye my hair, change my wardrobe or lose weight.

Sojourner Truth: If women want any more rights than they have, why don't they just take them, and not be talking about it.

Diane Sawyer: Whatever you want in life other people are going to want, too. Believe in yourself enough to accept the idea that you have an equal right to it.

Lily Tomlin: Sometimes I worry about being a success in a mediocre world.

LURVE YOURSELF

Jane White: Women should learn to be self-centred, and that's not the same as selfish, in the workplace. Because the workplace is lucky to have them.

Nellie McClung: Women who set a low value on themselves make life hard for all women.

Joan Rivers: Most people who are as attractive, witty and intelligent as I am are usually conceited.

Whitney Houston: I do like myself. In fact, I love me to death.

Marge Piercy: Love as if you liked yourself, and it may happen.

Lucille Ball: Love yourself first and everything else falls into line. You really have to love yourself to get anything done in this world.

EQUALITY ? THAT'S JUST LACK OF AMBITION

Marlo Thomas: A man has to be Joe McCarthy to be called ruthless. All a woman has to do is to put you on hold.

Charlotte Whitton: Whatever women do they must do twice as well as men to be thought half as good. Luckily, this is not difficult.

Olga Knopf: The art of being a woman can never consist of being a bad imitation of a man.

Wilma Scott Heide: The only jobs for which no man is qualified are human incubators and wet nurse. Likewise, the only job for which no woman is or can be qualified is sperm donor.

Bette Davis: When a man gives his opinion he's a man. When a woman gives her opinion she's a bitch.

Lois Wayne: Men are taught to apologize for their weaknesses, women for their strengths.

Anita Loos: The people I'm furious with are the women's liberationists. They keep getting up on soap boxes and proclaiming that women are brighter than men. It's true but it should be kept quiet or it ruins the whole racket.

Sarah Moore Grimke: I ask no favours for my sex . . . all I ask of our brethren is that they will take their feet off our necks.

Marlo Thomas: One of the things about equality is not just that you be treated equally to a man, but that you treat yourself equally to the way you treat a man.

Barbra Streisand: You don't ask a man, 'Do you want to be in control (of your job)?' You *assume* he wants control. Why would a woman be any different?

Margaret Hillis (conductor): There's only one woman I know who could never be a symphony conductor, and that's the Venus de Milo.

Dianne Feinstein
(*Democratic candidate*): Women are beginning to feel that they are not fairly represented . . .
2 per cent may be fine for fat in milk, but not for the United States Senate.

Charlotte Perkins Gilman:
There is no female mind. The brain is not an organ of sex. Might as well speak of a female liver.

SING IF YOU'RE GLAD
TO BE GREY

Julie Kavner: I feel that you reach a certain age and then things start to jell. My sense of self is stronger. I'm getting bolder in my old age. After I hit forty, you couldn't mess around with me so much anymore.

Lucille Ball: The secret of staying young is to live honestly, eat slowly, and lie about your age.

Frances Lear: I believe the second half of one's life is meant to be better than the first half. The first half is finding out how you do it. And the second half is enjoying it.

Raquel Welch: Change excites me. I am fifty years old. It's when the mind catches up with the body.

Helen Hayes (aged 84): The hardest years in life are those between ten and seventy.

Billie Burke: Age is something that doesn't matter, unless you are a cheese.

Brett Butler: The older I get, the simpler the definition of maturity seems: it's the length of time between when I realize someone is a jackass and when I tell them that they're one.

Anon: You're only young once - after that you need another excuse.

—

Rose, (The Golden Girls): My mother used to say: the older you get, the better you get - unless you're a banana.

Virginia Woolf: The older one grows, the more one likes indecency.

Carolyn Heilbrun: Once women pass fifty, if they can avoid the temptations of the eternal youth purveyors, the sellers of unnatural thinness and cosmetic surgery, they may be able to tap into the feisty girls they once were.

Cathy Ladman: My grandmother's ninety. She's dating. He's ninety-three. It's going great. They never argue. They can't hear each other.

Rita Rudner: I don't plan to grow old gracefully. I plan to have face-lifts till my ears meet.

Lynn Hall: We did not change as we grew older; we just became more clearly ourselves.

Ellen Degeneres: My grandmother started walking five miles a day when she was sixty. She's ninety-three today and we don't know where the hell she is.

Gloria Steinem: It doesn't really matter whether sex goes or doesn't go. What matters is that the older woman can choose whether it goes or not.

Cathleen Rountree: Ageism is a final frontier, the last metaphorical girdle from which women must free themselves.

Brigitte Bardot: It is sad to grow old but nice to ripen.

Ethel Payne: Age is not a handicap. Age is nothing but a number. It is how you use it.

Dorothy L. Sayers: Time and trouble will tame any advanced young woman, but an advanced old woman is uncontrollable by any earthly force.

Emmylou Harris: I'm proud (my hair) is completely grey, and I'm not going to bother with colouring it because I have other things to do with my time. Also, I like the way it looks. If it encourages other women to say, 'I can do that, too,' that's great, and they should wear it proudly. We earned those grey hairs!

Susan Sarandon: I look forward to being older, when what you look like becomes less and less the issue and what you are is the point.

Alta: Little old ladies is the term they use to make us laugh at the women who have been fighting for sixty years.

Diane de Poitiers:
The years that a woman subtracts
from her age are not lost. They
are added to other women's.

Ellen West: I am twenty-one
years old and am supposed to be
silent and grin like a puppet.

Jane Fonda: I'm forty-six years old, and if you look at the history of ageing actresses, it's not exactly a bright future. I intend, of course, to change that.

Ginger Rogers: Youth is in the mind, not in the condition of your flesh.

Kim Basinger: When I'm old I'm never going to say, 'I didn't do this' or, 'I regret that'. I'm going to say, 'I don't regret a damn thing. I came, I went, and I did it all'.

FAT IS A FATUOUS ISSUE

Roseanne: Women should try to increase their size rather than decrease it, because I believe the bigger we are, the more space we'll take up, and the more we'll have to be reckoned with. I think every woman should be fat like me.

Kim Chernin: A woman obsessed with her body is also obsessed with the limitations of her emotional life.

Carol Leifer: I'm not into working out. My philosophy: no pain, no pain.

Monica Piper: I went to a conference for bulimics and anorexics...the bulimics ate the anorexics.

Mae West: I never worry about diets. The only carrots that interest me are the number you get in a diamond.

Paula Poundstone: I've decided that perhaps I'm bulimic and just keep forgetting to purge.

TROUBLE AND STRIFE

Katharine Hepburn:
Sometimes I wonder if men and women suit each other. Perhaps they should live next door and just visit now and then.

Mae West: Marriage is a great institution, but I'm not ready for an institution yet.

Joan Rivers: My mother gave me this advice: Trust your husband, adore your husband and get as much as you can in your own name.

Germaine Greer: Marriage . . . cannot . . . offer emotional security, for such security is the achievement of the individual.

Phyllis Diller: Never go to bed mad. Stay up and fight.

Adela Rogers St John: There is so little difference between husbands you might as well keep the first.

Anon: Husbands are living proof that women have a sense of humour.

Mae West: Don't marry a man to reform him - that's what reform schools are for.

Gloria Steinem: I have yet to hear a man ask for advice on how to combine marriage and a career.

Rita Rudner: My grandmother was a very tough woman. She buried three husbands. Two of them were just napping.

Jean Kerr: Personally, I think if a woman hasn't met the right man by the time she's twenty-four, she may be lucky.

Phyllis Diller: Fang and I are always fighting. When we get up in the morning, we don't kiss; we touch gloves.

Barbara Lazear Ascher: Infidelity is reason enough for gun control.

Marsha Warfield: Kids are like husbands - they're fine as long as they're someone else's.

Helen Rowland: When you see what some girls marry, you realize how they must hate to work for a living.

Isadora Duncan: Any intelligent woman who reads the marriage contract, and then goes into it, deserves all the consequences.

Anon: I still miss my ex-husband (but my aim is improving).

Susanna Moodie: I have no wish for a second husband. I had enough of the first. I like to have my own way - to lie down mistress, and get up master.

Zsa Zsa Gabor: I never hated a man enough to give him back his diamonds.

Marion Smith: One of the advantages of living alone is that you don't have to wake up in the arms of a loved one.

Anon: One of the surest signs that a woman is in love is when she divorces her husband.

Andra Douglas: The only thing that keeps me from being happily married . . . is my husband.

Nancy Astor: I married beneath me - all women do.

I HATE HOUSEWORK

Joan Rivers: Don't cook. Don't clean. No man will ever make love to a woman because she waxed the linoleum - 'My God, the floor's immaculate. Lie down you hot bitch.'

Roseanne: I don't like to be called a 'housewife' . . . I prefer 'domestic goddess'.

Joan Rivers: I hate housework! You make the beds, you do the dishes - and six months later you have to start all over again.

Zsa Zsa Gabor: I am a marvellous housekeeper. Every time I leave a man I keep his house.

Anna Quinlin: When men do dishes it's called helping. When women do dishes it's called life.

Letty Cottin Pogrebin: No labourer in the world is expected to work for room, board and love - except the housewife.

Erma Bombeck: Housework can kill you if done right.

Roseanne: When Sears comes out with a riding vacuum cleaner, then I'll clean the house.

Liz Scott: A dish that don't survive the dishwasher don't deserve to live.

Anne Gibbons: Nature abhors a vacuum and so do I.

ONLY SKIN DEEP

Sharon Stone: I don't believe make-up and the right hairstyle alone can make a woman beautiful. The most radiant woman in the room is the one most full of life and experience.

Hedy Lamarr: Any girl can be glamorous. All you have to do is stand still and look stupid.

Henriette Mantel: I don't have the time every day to put on make-up. I need that time to clean my rifle.

MEN, WHO NEEDS THEM!

Dorothy Parker: I require only three things of a man. He must be handsome, ruthless and stupid.

Rita Rudner: I was a ballerina. I had to quit after I injured a groin muscle. It wasn't mine.

Lynn Hecht Schafren: Why is it that men can be bastards and women must wear pearls and smile?

Rhonda Dickison: If you love someone, set them free. If they come back, they're probably broke.

Angela Martin:
Q: What do you do when your boyfriend walks out?
A: Shut the door.

Jay Behar: I'm at a point where I want a man in my life - but not in my house! Just come in, attach the VCR, and get out.

Roseanne: A guy is a lump like a doughnut. So, first you gotta get rid of all the stuff his mum did to him, and then you gotta get rid of all that macho crap that they pick up from the beer commercials. And then there's my personal favourite, the male ego.

Cynthia Heimel: A woman needs a man like a fish needs a net.

Mamie Van Doren:
(on Warren Beatty) He's the type of man who will end up dying in his own arms.

Bette Davis: The male ego with few exceptions is elephantine to start with.

Nancy Astor: In passing, also, I would like to say that the first time Adam had a chance he laid the blame on woman.

Roseanne: Men can read maps better than women. 'Cause only the male mind could conceive of one inch equalling a hundred miles.

Donna Gephart: If brevity is the soul of wit, your penis must be a riot.

Judy Tenuta: How many of you ever started dating someone because you were too lazy to commit suicide?

Erika Ritter: I believe in women. Men are just unsubstantiated rumours.

Coco Chanel: As long as you know that most men are like children you know everything.

Raquel Welch: There aren't any hard women, only soft men.

Ruth Gordon: In our family we don't divorce our men - we bury them.

Margaret Mead: Women want mediocre men, and men are working hard to become as mediocre as possible.

Gloria Steinem:
(If men could menstruate)
sanitary supplies would be
federally funded and free. Of
course, some men would still pay
for the prestige of such
commercial brands as Paul
Newman Tampons, Muhammed
Ali's Rope-a-Dope Pads, John
Wayne Maxi Pads, and Joe
Namath Jock Shields - 'For
Those Light Bachelor Days'.

Roseanne: If men really knew how to do it, they wouldn't have to pay for it.

Cher: The trouble with some women is that they get all excited about nothing - and then marry him.

Jessica Tandy: When he's late for dinner, I know he's either having an affair or is lying dead in the street. I always hope it's the street.

Elaine Boosler: My ancestors wandered lost in the wilderness for forty years because even in biblical times, men would not stop to ask for directions.

Anon: How many men does it take to tile the floor? It depends how thin you slice them.

Anon: If they can put a man on the moon . . . why can't they put them all there?

Madonna: I wouldn't want a penis. It would be like a third leg. It would seem like a contraption that would get in your way.

Camille Paglia: There is no female Mozart because there is no female Jack the Ripper.

Katherine Anne Porter: It's a man's world, and you men can have it.

OO ER MISSUS!

Cynthia Heimel: All that you suspect about women's friendships is true. We talk about dick size.

Nora Ephron: In my sex fantasy, nobody ever loves me for my mind.

Tallulah Bankhead: If I had to live my life again, I'd make the same mistakes, only sooner.

Rita Mae Brown: Lead me not into temptation; I can find the way myself.

Shelley Winters: I have bursts of being a lady, but it doesn't last long.

Donna Gephart: I'd get into bondage, but there are too many strings attached.

Mae West: To err is human, but it feels divine.

Nancy Linn-Desmond: Easy is an adjective used to describe a woman who has the sexual morals of a man.

Jean Harlow: I like to wake up feeling a new man.

Leontyne Price: A healthy sex life. Best thing in the world for a woman's voice.

Lena Horne: Honey, sex doesn't stop until you're in the grave.

Mae West: She's the kind of girl who climbed the ladder of success, wrong by wrong.

Mae West: *(on being told there were ten men waiting to see her)* I'm tired. Send one of them home.

Cher: A girl can wait for the right man to come along but in the meantime that still doesn't mean she can't have a wonderful time with all the wrong ones.

Joan Rivers: It's been so long since I made love, I can't even remember who gets tied up.

Anon: So many men and so many reasons not to sleep with any of them.

Mae West: It's not the men in my life that count, it's the life in my men.

Moms Mabley: An old man can't do nothing for me except bring me a message from a young man.

Sophia Loren: Sex appeal is 50 per cent what you've got and 50 per cent what people think you've got.

Mae West: I feel like a million tonight, but one at a time.

Katharine Hepburn: Plain women know more about men than beautiful ones do.

NO PAIN, NO GAIN

Bernice Johnson Reagon:
Life's challenges are not supposed
to paralyse you, they're supposed
to help you discover who you are.

Beverley Sills: You may be
disappointed if you fail, but you
are doomed if you don't try.

Edith Wharton: If only we'd stop trying to be happy we'd have a pretty good time.

Nancy Reagan: A woman is like a tea bag. It's only when she's in hot water that you realize how strong she is.

Golda Meir: Those who do not know how to weep with their whole heart don't know how to laugh either.

Libby Riddles
(sled-dog race winner):
I don't know why it should surprise people women are so tough. What I do is probably not as tough as (being) a single mother, raising two kids and paying rent or a mortgage.

Edith Wharton: Life is either always a tightrope or a feather bed. Give me the tightrope.

Sophia Loren: Mistakes are part of the dues one pays for a full life.

Rosalind Russell: Flops are part of life's menu and I've never been a girl to miss out on any of the courses.

Joan Collins: Show me a person who has never made a mistake and I'll show you somebody who has never achieved much.

Katherine Mansfield: When we can begin to take our failures nonseriously, it means we are ceasing to be afraid of them.

Carolyn See: If you try and fail that's better than saying, I could have written it if I hadn't married Harold.

TAKE CONTROL

Jeanette Rankin: As a woman I cannot go to war, and I refuse to send anyone else.

Wilma Vaught *(Brigadier General of the US Air Force):* What I wanted to be when I grew up was - in charge.

Carrie Snow: If women ruled the world and we all got massages, there would be no war.

Patricia Schroeder
(Congresswoman):
When people ask me why I am running as a woman, I always answer, 'What choice do I have?'

Catherine the Great:
Do you know, it is not praise that
does me good, but when men
speak ill of me, then, with a noble
assurance I say to myself, as I
smile at them, 'Let us be revenged
by proving them to be liars.'

Maureen Murphy: The reason there are so few female politicians is that it is too much trouble to put make-up on two faces.

Susan B. Anthony: The true republic: men, their rights and nothing more; women, their rights and nothing less.

Margaret Thatcher:
In politics, if you want anything said, ask a man; if you want anything done, ask a woman.

Claire Sargent: I think it's about time we voted for senators with breasts. After all, we've been voting for boobs long enough.

KIDS, WHO NEEDS 'EM!

Cher: I have a lot of friends who are bringing up their children alone. Men are not a necessity. You don't need them to live. You don't have to have them to survive.

June Jordan: ... everybody's momma done better than anybody had any right to expect she would. And that's the truth.

Princess of Wales:
My husband knows so much about rearing children that I've suggested he has the next one and I'll sit back and give advice.

Florynce Kenney: If men could get pregnant, abortion would be a sacrament.

Roseanne: Hey, the way I figure it is this: if the kids are still alive by the time my husband comes home, I've done my job.

WISE WOMEN

Wilma Scott Heide: We whose hands have rocked the cradle are now using our heads to rock the boat.

Judy Tenuta: It's hard to be nice to some paranoid schizophrenic just because she lives in your body.

Alice Roosevelt Longworth:
I have a simple philosophy. Fill what's empty. Empty what's full, and scratch where it itches.

Lily Tomlin: Reality is a crutch for people who can't cope with drugs.

Gertrude Stein: Everything is so dangerous that nothing is really very frightening.

Jodie Foster: I'm really sick of people apologizing for feminism as if it would leave nasty stains. Feminism is one of the greatest humanisms. It's about making the world more human.

Simone de Beauvoir:
On the day when it will be
possible for woman to love not in
her weakness but in her strength,
not to escape herself but to find
herself, not to abase herself but to
assert herself - on that day love
will become for her, as for man, a
source of life and not of mortal
danger.

Anne Morrow Lindbergh:
What a commentary on our civilization, when being alone is considered suspect; when one has to apologize for it, make excuses, hide the fact that one practices it - like a secret vice.

I WILL SURVIVE

Shirley MacLaine: I don't need a man to rectify my existence. The most profound relationship we'll ever have is the one with ourselves.

Beverley Sills: There is a growing strength in women - but it's in the forehead, not the forearm.

Jenny Holzer: Expiring for love is beautiful but stupid.

Gilda Radner: Whether you're married or not, whether you have a boyfriend or not, there is no real security except for whatever you build inside yourself.

Anjelica Huston: I've always had a little contempt for women who marry because they want to be looked after in their old age. I always thought one should be rich oneself.

Michelle Pfeiffer: I find the less you focus on (your flaws), the better off you are. Be yourself and be glad of who you are.

Maya Angelou: It can be a great idea, this concept of courage. It is the most important of all virtues, because without it we can't practise any other virtue with consistency.

Marlo Thomas: Any woman who accepts aloneness as the natural by-product of success is accepting the punishment for a crime she didn't commit.

Cindy Crawford: I'm a woman; I'm not ashamed or embarrassed or afraid of it. What *woman* means to me is gentle, sexy and solid.

Jane Fonda: It's never too late - never too late to start over, never too late to be happy.

George Eliot: It is never too late to be what you might have been.

Pearl S. Buck: Inside myself is a place where I live all alone and that's where you renew your springs that never dry up.

Anaïs Nin: Life shrinks or expands according to one's courage.

Ingrid Bergman: I have no regrets. I wouldn't have lived my life the way I did if I was going to worry about what people were going to say.

Helen Keller: Keep your face to the sunshine and you cannot see the shadow.

Susan Jeffers: Feel the fear, and do it anyway.

Margaret Thatcher: I always cheer up immensely if an attack is particularly wounding because I think, well, if they attack me personally, it means they have not a single political argument left.

Molly Ivins: Whatever you do, don't give up. Because all you can do once you've given up is bitch. I've known some great bitches in my time. With some it's a passion, with others an art.

Eleanor Roosevelt: You must do the thing you think you cannot do.

Marie Curie: Nothing in life is to be feared, it is only to be understood.

Gloria Steinem: We need to demystify the forces that have told us what we *should* be before we can value what we *are*.

Rosalynn Carter: You have to have confidence in your ability, and then be tough enough to follow through.

Laurie Kuslansky: Laugh and the world laughs with you. Cry and you cry with your girlfriends.

Fran Lebowitz: It's not whether you win or lose - it's how you lay the blame.

Fay Weldon: Worry less about what other people think about you, and more about what you think of them.

Rachel Hickerson: I may not be making a living, but I'm making a difference.

Mary Frances Connelly: Life's a bitch and then they call you one.

Please contact our Sales Department for a
FREE catalogue, containing information on
other titles published by

MICHAEL O'MARA BOOKS LIMITED
9 Lion Yard
Tremadoc Road
London SW4 7NQ
Tel: 0171-720-8643
Fax: 0171-627-8953